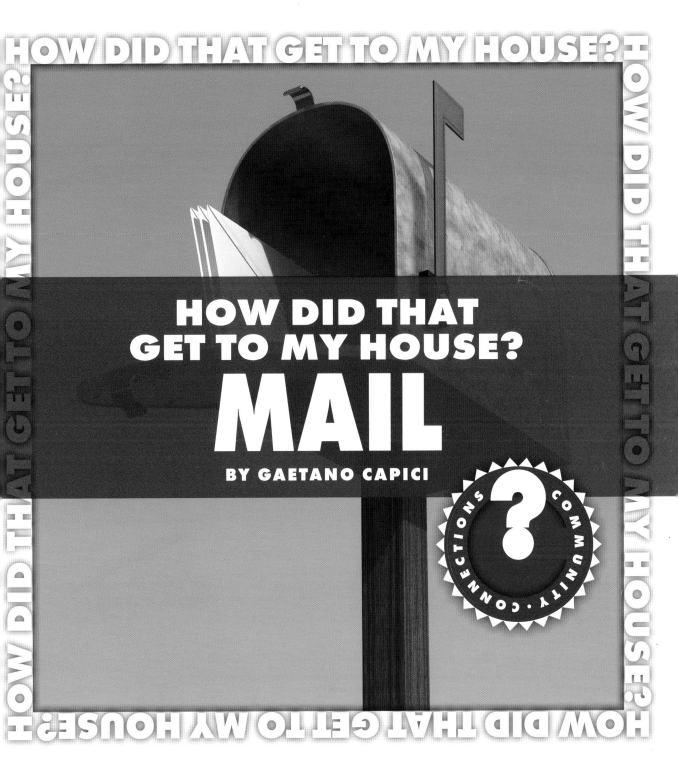

HOW DID THAT GET TO MY HOUSE?
MAIL

BY GAETANO CAPICI

COMMUNITY · CONNECTIONS ?

HOW DID THAT GET TO MY HOUSE?

CHERRY LAKE
Publishing

Published in the United States of America by Cherry Lake Publishing
Ann Arbor, Michigan
www.cherrylakepublishing.com

Content Adviser: Katrina Ramos, Director of the Student Post Office,
Clemson University, Clemson, South Carolina
Reading Adviser: Cecilia Minden-Cupp, PhD, Literacy Consultant

Photo Credits: Cover and page 1, ©James Steidl, used under license from Shutterstock, Inc.;
page 5, ©Cheryl Casey, used under license from Shutterstock, Inc.; page 7, ©Scott A. Frangos,
used under license from Shutterstock, Inc.; pages 9 and 11, ©David R. Frazier Photolibrary, Inc./
Alamy; page 13, ©JoLin, used under license from Shutterstock, Inc.; page 15, ©jeff Metzger,
used under license from Shutterstock, Inc.; page 17, ©Ivan Cholakov, used under license from
Shutterstock, Inc.; page 19, ©iStockphoto.com/Captainflash; page 21, ©Tom Tracy
Photography/Alamy

LIBRARY OF CONGRESS CATALOGING-IN-PUBLICATION DATA
Capici, Gaetano, 1985-
  How did that get to my house? Mail / by Gaetano Capici.
     p. cm.—(Community connections)
  Includes index.
  ISBN-13: 978-1-60279-478-8
  ISBN-10: 1-60279-478-2
  1. Postal service—United States—Juvenile literature. 2. United States Postal Service—
Juvenile literature. I. Title. II. Series.
  HE6371.C37 2010
  383'.4973—dc22   2008046012

Cherry Lake Publishing would like to acknowledge the
work of The Partnership for 21st Century Skills. Please
visit www.21stcenturyskills.org for more information.

CONTENTS

IT'S PICK-UP TIME!

"There, that's the last one," Stella said to her dad. She dropped the final envelope into the mailbox. "Will my friends get these invitations today?"

"Probably not," her father responded. "Remember that mail goes through many steps before someone receives it. Don't worry, it won't take too long."

Sending mail is a fun way to stay in touch with family and friends.

5

The U.S. Postal Service (USPS) handles mail in the United States. Have you ever seen a blue mailbox on the street? That is one place where people put mail they want to send.

People can bring mail to the **post office**. You can also leave mail in your home mailbox. A mail carrier will take it when she brings your family's mail.

Mail carriers use keys to unlock mailboxes. Why do you think mailboxes are locked?

Mail carriers collect the mail. They take it from mailboxes. They put the mail in their trucks. Carriers take the mail to a post office.

Mail is sorted at the **processing center**. This is a big building with special machines and workers. Let's find out how the machines and workers sort mail.

Mail carriers use large containers to hold the mail they collect.

SORTING ALL THAT MAIL

At the processing center, the mail is placed on **conveyor belts**. The belts move the mail from one machine to the next.

Workers and machines separate letters from large envelopes and packages. The letters pass through a machine. It makes sure the letters face the same direction.

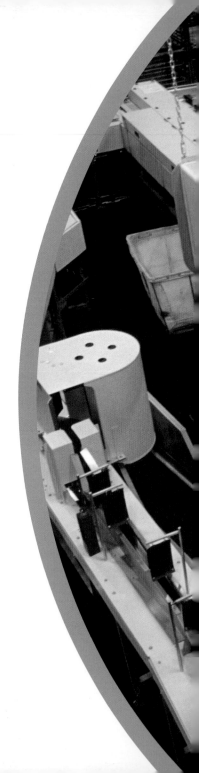

Machines help workers sort the mail.

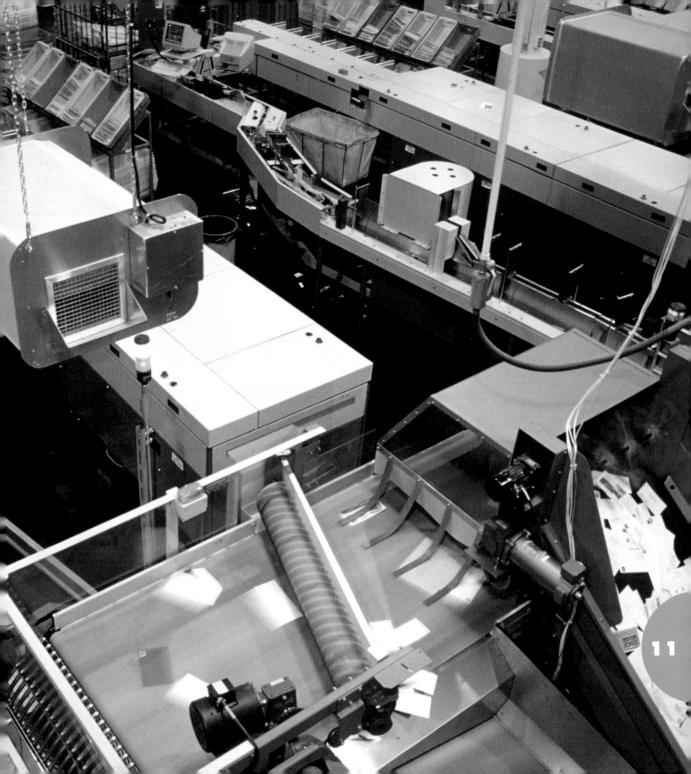

11

You can use a stamp only one time. The machine **cancels** the stamp by putting a special mark over it. Now you cannot use the stamp again. The machine also puts a **postmark** on the letter. The postmark shows where and when the letter was mailed.

Can you see the mark that shows this stamp has already been used?

THINK!

Canceling a stamp makes it easy to tell if the stamp was used. Why do you think stamps are only used once? Here's a hint: stamps help pay the costs of sending mail.

13

Then a machine prints a **bar code** on each envelope. Bar codes are special marks. They match the **zip code** where the mail is going.

Another machine reads the bar codes. It separates the letters into bins. Mail going to different places goes into different bins.

Bar codes help workers know where each letter must go.

Look at a letter your family received in the mail. Take a good look at the envelope. Do you see the bar code? Do you see the postmark? Can you tell where the letter was mailed?

Packages are not handled the same way as letters. Workers use computers and machines made for handling packages.

The sorted mail is put into big trucks. Some trucks bring mail to nearby post offices. Other trucks head for the airport. That mail will travel by plane. It will go to other cities, states, or countries.

Airplanes carry mail that must travel long distances.

YOU HAVE MAIL!

Mail comes to the post office after it arrives in the correct town. Now the mail is sorted again. It must be separated into different **routes**. A route includes all the houses and buildings where a mail carrier delivers mail. Each carrier delivers mail to a different part of town. That is his or her route.

A mail carrier delivers mail by truck.

Some mail carriers walk from mailbox to mailbox. They carry the mail in a bag. Others use cars or small trucks. They all put the mail into the correct mailbox.

Check your mailbox. Do you have mail? Now you know how it got there!

Have you met your mail carrier? The same person delivers your mail almost every day.

How big is your town? Guess how many pieces of mail are delivered in your town each day. Visit the post office. Ask a postal worker to give you an estimate. How close was your guess?

GLOSSARY

bar code (BAR KOHD) a set of lines containing information read by machines

cancels (KAN-suhlz) prints a mark over a postage stamp so that it cannot be used again

conveyor belts (kuhn-VAY-ur BELTSS) moving surfaces that bring objects from one place to another

postmark (POHST-mark) a special marking that shows when and where a letter was mailed

post office (POHST OF-iss) a building or place where stamps are sold and mail is organized

processing center (PROSS-ess-ing SEN-tur) large building where workers use machines to sort mail for delivery

routes (ROOTSS) groups of houses and buildings where mail carriers go to deliver mail

zip code (ZIP KOHD) a number that the Postal Service gives to each delivery area in the United States

FIND OUT MORE

BOOKS

Knudsen, Shannon. *Postal Workers*. Minneapolis: Lerner Publications Company, 2005.

Minden, Cecilia. *Letter Carriers*. Chanhassen, MN: The Child's World, 2006.

WEB LINKS

USPS—Addressing Tips & Tools

www.usps.com/send/preparemailandpackages/labelsandaddressing/usingthecorrectaddress.htm
Check out diagrams and tips on how to correctly address your letters and other mail

USPS—Postal Facts

www.usps.com/communications/newsroom/postalfacts.htm
Learn how much mail the United States Postal Service processes and delivers every day

INDEX

ABOUT THE AUTHOR

Gaetano Capici graduated from DePaul University with bachelor's degrees in English and Spanish. This is his first children's book. After researching this title, he has a deeper appreciation for the postal system. He lives near Chicago, Illinois.

24